Ascension KIS

Opening *The* Doorways *To* Light

Words & *Illustration*

Shima Shanti   **James Gordon Kelly IV**

Peace Waters Publishing
San Diego, CA 92128

Ascension Kis
Opening the Doorways to Light

Edited by Barbara McNichol Editorial, www.BarbaraMcNichol.com

Publishing Consultant, Project Manager, and Book Interior Layout by Karen Saunders, MacGraphics Services, http://www.macgraphics.net

Cover Illustration and Design by Mike Clark

Illustrated by James Gordon Kelly IV

ISBN 978-0-9915481-0-1
Library of Congress Control Number 2014902702

Printed in the United States of America
Second Printing April 2014
Lightning Source Printers

Published by
Peace Waters Publishing
San Diego, CA 92128
www.peacewaters.com

I'm So Grateful—Dedicated to YOU!

I dedicate Peace Waters, *Ascension Kis,* and all the books in the Journey OM Series to *YOU*. Thank you for allowing your God Presence to guide you and for your willingness to experience life as Grace, Peace, and Harmony. Your dedication to your spiritual evolvement is a gift to the enlightenment of us all. By opening this book you have acknowledged your Higher Self and have allowed yourself the opportunity to live life as Spirit in human form, embracing all aspects of your Divine Self.

And, to *you* my beloved husband, Jim, I dearly dedicate all of the joy and abundance that is Peace Waters. It is with Love that knows no bounds that I share all of me with you. You are my *Heaven on Earth* who, for thirty-eight years, has held the tether so I may soar in the celestial realms.

Shimia

"Peace I leave with you; My Peace I give to you."

I am in joy and delight that you have found your way
to the Ascension Kis and the divine gifts
I am guided to share.

To Thy Will Be True.
Peace All Ways,

Shimia

March 2014

Contents

Introduction
The Evolution of Ascension Kis

Welcome! You have opened the pages to the Second Edition of the *Ascension Kis: Opening the Doorways to Light*. This book represents both *my* spiritual evolution and *yours*.

The Ascension Kis originated in 2007 in a channeled session with my friend Judith K. Moore. We were brought together in a contract made beyond lifetimes in which she agreed to be the messenger who would remind me of my calling as an Ascension wayshower. She gave me just enough clues to inspire me to create tools for Ascension. Thus Peace Waters was born.

Judith can *see* and *read* Light Language. In our channeled sessions, she shared her gift of seeing the radiance of Light. After each meeting, I would end up with pages of her drawings that looked to me like squiggly lines and scribbles. Encouraging me to own my Divinity and fulfill my soul purpose, Judith suggested I *make something* of these primitive designs. And so I did.

At first there were three: Wisdom, Grace, and Discernment. I made elaborate tiny silk packets containing Celtic sea salt that people could carry in their pockets or put under their pillows. I called them *Energy Packets*. To infuse each with a spiritual frequency of Wisdom, Grace, and Discernment, I ceremonially placed each symbol in a singing crystal bowl filled with sea salt and gemstones, and then I toned its sacred vibration into the vibrating vessel. Each salt packet came with a card printed with the primitive glyph and my description of Wisdom, Grace, and Discernment. They were ready!

Next, I did all the things I knew as a professional businesswoman to market these extraordinary products. I created a website and shopping cart to offer my Peace Waters inspirations. I listed them on eBay and tried to sell them through traditional retail channels. All with no success.

As beautiful and miraculous as the Ascension Kis/Keys were to me, I began to give them away, rationalizing that "it simply wasn't time." But with them, I had planted a seed, and that was good. So I stored the packets along with my ambitions and moved on to travel on soul journeys—The Chief Joseph Trail and Lake Louise. I also began writing.

It was years later when I realized the Ascension Kis/Keys represented *my* process of enlightenment. They took me to the place of Creation I can only describe as pure joy. And in that place of Bliss, immense gifts of illumination were bestowed on me. They had awakened me and that was enough; that was their purpose (or so I thought).

Eventually, more Kis/Keys were revealed. Three became fifteen. With renewed enthusiasm, I tried again to share these mystical symbols commercially. I searched for an illustrator and found one close to home—our son Jimmy—who was just awakening to his own divine gifts through art and sacred geometry. So I did the writing, Jimmy did the drawing, and together we created our First Edition and a deck of cards.

Back then, I called them "Ascension Keys." I only knew *ki* as the English word *key*, not a vibration. But this was enough to open my consciousness and grasp the gift of these profound symbols. With greater understanding, I realized *ki* is a sound, not a word; it's a mantra similar to the Universal sound om. Previously, I only could comprehend *key* as a device used to unlock something. However, its meaning opened my consciousness so I could grasp the spiritual Wisdom of these little glyphs.

The printed First Edition of *Ascension Keys: Divine Principles in the Language of Light* was ready to make its way into the hands of spiritual seekers. Again, no paying hands reached out for it, so I gave them away to friends—mostly to Judith for her speaking engagements and work with students. Each person who connected with the kis experienced amazing shifts in consciousness. For me, these divine tools affirmed my connection to God and deepened my understanding of Ascension.

I realized it was the Creation that expanded my joy of knowing God and who I AM. I am free of expectation for financial gain or celebrity. Rather, my reward comes in sharing with you. This is *my* spiritual journey, my pure expression of joy. It reflects where I am closest to my Heart and my God within.

And now in your hands is the Second Edition of the *Ascension Kis: Opening the Doorways to Light*. It is a collection of the originals that has expanded to include thirty-three Ascension glyphs. You may notice a watermark on some of the pages but not all. Each watermark is my tribute to the original *Keys* and honors the beginning of Judith's, Jimmy's, and my cocreation. Each one symbolizes ever-flowing transformations and possibilities. They awakened me to my God Presence and always accompany me on my spiritual journey. Perhaps they will be your awakening, too.

This Second Edition is an expression of my level of consciousness *now*. Visions of a future memory tell me I have more to discover and learn and share! More important, I am guided to let flow all of the gifts I've received in certain moments of time, even the ones I've left behind. And rather than pack them away, I'm blessed to share them with you. Perhaps they will touch you like they did me on your journey of Ascension.

I wish for you to *discover* the joy of who you truly are in the pages of the *Ascension Kis* that follow. In that, I will feel delighted.

To Thy Will Always be True. Peace All Ways.

Ascension Kis

Allow

I AM the Serenity of Allowance.

Harmonizes with the Threefold Flame

Love, Wisdom, and Power

In Flow

Opens to Universal Wisdom

Lives Life in Love

Transforms Resistance into Grace and Serenity

Is Grace in Action—*Thy Will Be Done*

Is the Ki to Freedom

Trust

Thy Will Be Done.

Surrenders to the Union of self and Divine Self

Believes in God

Manifests Universal Law

Is Life Conceived of Love

Thy Will and my Will are One

Truth

I AM the Absolute.

Is Ever Present, Transparent, and Immutable

Expands God Consciousness

Originates from Oneness

Is the Essence of Creation

Is the Immaculate Conception

Discernment

I AM Universal Order.

Aligns Free Will with Thy Will

Trusts Intuition

Perceives Truth

Is Mindful

Listens to the Still Small Voice Within

Harmony (I)

I AM the Harmony of Universal Light.

In Balance with Universal Law

Is Equipoise—Fullness

Is Sacred Resonance

Conceives Perfect Oneness

Harmony (II)

I AM Sacred Resonance.

Is Grace

The Sound of Light

Music of the Spheres

Intention

I AM the Passion of Ascension.

Unites Mind and Heart

Ignites, Conceives, and Initiates Ascension

Is Passion

Office of the Christ

As Above, So Below.

A Station of Ascension

A Place of Being

The Consciousness of Perfect Desire, Thought, and Intention

The Convergence of Ascension and descension

The Redemptive Office of Divine Life

The Alchemy of Creation

Christ Consciousness—Unconditional Love

Authorship

I AM the Soul of God.

Translates Thought and Geometry into Language
Receives and Conveys Divine Thought
Creates Templates to Commune with God
Illumines the Light of Sacred Geometry
Is the Power to Manifest the Word of God

Discipline

I AM the Disciple.

Harmonizes Thought into Order

Accepts the Truth of God Consciousness

Exemplifies *Thy Will* through Intention and Action

Opens a Portal to God—a Pathway to Ascension

Forgiveness

I AM the Mirror of Divine Truth.

Allows, Accepts, and Receives

Embraces Everyone, Everything in Grace

Surrenders to Divine Purpose

Resonates in Oneness

Mirrors the Divine

Is Unconditional Love

Manifestation

I AM the Idea of God in Form.

Aligns Intent and Purpose in Perfect Creation

Is the Immaculate Concept in Form

Receives Inspiration through the Heart

Is One with Universal Law

Freedom

I AM Liberty.

Transcends Belief that Ownership Gives Power

Releases Boundaries of Duality

Frees Spirit to Flow in Universal Life

Confers the Generosity of Compassion

Knows *I AM* Son of God

Is Liberty

Gratitude

I AM Grateful!

Appreciates *All That Is*

Opens to Unconditional Love

Seeds Compassion

Expresses All Blessings of Life

Abides in Grace

The Conception of Peace

The Dwelling Place of Divine Self

Grace

I AM the I of God.

Serenity, Poise, and Dignity
Opulence, Beauty, Perfection, and Balance
The Harmony of Heaven—The Harmony of Peace
Opens to the Elohim and Archangelic Realms
The Holy Spirit Manifest
The Similitude of God
All Divine Gifts within One

Reciprocity

I AM the Circle of Creation.

Gift Given—Gift Received

Transformations—Possibilities

Conceives Thought in Oneness

The Circle of Universal Flow

Is a Ki to Peace

Creation — God in Form

I AM God.

Links to Multidimensional Realities
Dwells in the Field of Nothingness—*All That Is*
Is the Sacred Geometry of Light and Love
The Trinity Begets the Circle
Father, Son, and Holy Spirit are One

Wisdom

I AM the One All Knowing Mind and Heart.

Awakens Divine Purpose

Illumines

Mind and Heart are One

Is the Omniscient Mind of God

All-Knowing

The Way of Ascension

Bliss — Celebration

I AM Light.

All is within Self

The Stillness of Peace

The Effervescence of Light and Love

Dancing with Angels

Heart

I AM the Sacred Heart of Infinity.

The Seat of Divinity

The Rhythm of Soul

He—Art

The Chalice of Wisdom

The Threefold Flame

Love

I AM the Spiral of Love Ever and Eternal.

Is Oneness

Union with I AM

Manifests Grace

Knows Thine Own Truth

The Living Body

All That Is

God

Majesty

I AM the Majesty of the Mind of God.

Illuminates the Divine Light Body

Awakens Higher Self, God Presence, I AM

The Origin of Divinity

The Divine Masculine

Pure Beingness

Patience

I AM Now in the Divine Moment. I AM Presence.

Experiences Each Moment with Divine Purpose

Divine Timing—*Thy Will*

Trusts Divine Order

Surrenders to the Moment of Creation

Allows Manifest Perfection

Is Presence—Now

All That Is Every Moment

Sacred Resonance

I AM the Song of Creation.

Harmony of Body, Soul, and Spirit
Attunes the Light Body to the Universal Om
Music of the Spheres

Star of David Tetrahedron

I AM the Harmony of All.

Mind and Heart in Oneness

Heaven on Earth

All That Is—As Above, So Below

Universe

I AM of God.

The Assembly of Light

Creation of The Elohim

Father God and Divine Mother Manifest through the Holy Spirit

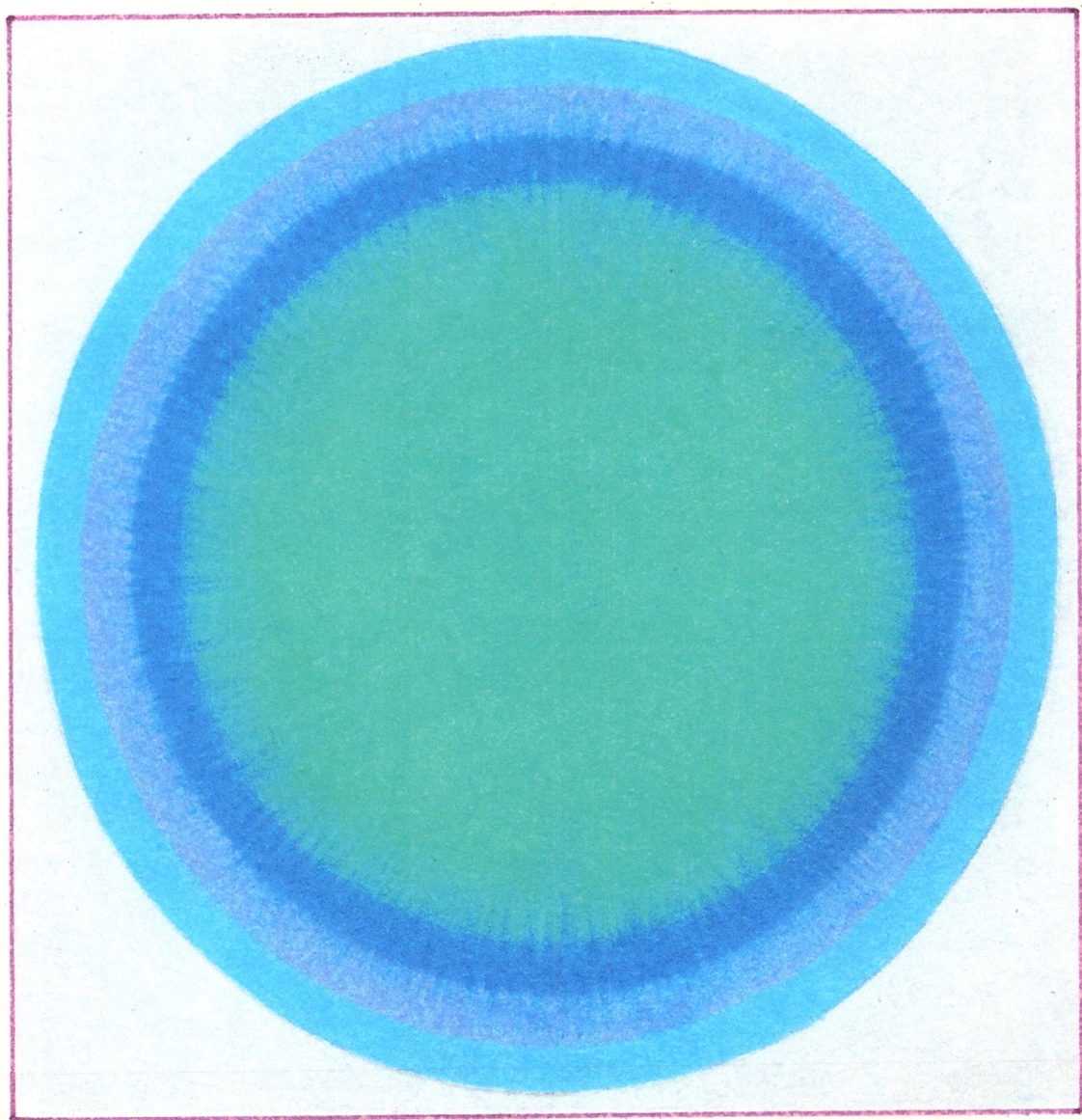

Divinity (I)

I AM in the World, Not of the World.

Opens the Heart to Spiritual Realms

The Union of Self and Source

Likeness of God

Divinity (II)

I AM One.

Flows in Infinite Oneness
Spirals in Circles of Light
In Perfect Similitude

I AM

I AM.

Perceives Self Beyond Human

Wisdom, Oneness, and Harmony

Final Convergence of Body, Mind, and Soul

Opens to Ascension

Self-Love

Oneness

I AM Universal Consciousness.

Leads to the Eternal Om

All Truth

The Immaculate Conception

Universal Consciousness

Unalterable Law, Immutable Light, and Absolute Love

OM

I AM, Auhm, Om.

Is the Supreme Sound of the Universe
Constant, Forever, and Eternal
Alpha & Omega, without Beginning or End
Attunes All Vibration to Source
Ignites the Expression of Love
The Essence of Creation
The Song of the Soul
The Harmony of One
All I AM
Oneness

Peace

I AM the Harmony of Peace.

The Sanctity of Oneness

Harmony, Grace, and Gratitude

Dwells in Balance

The Still Voice Within

The Sacred Heart

Ascension

I AM Home in Eternal Oneness.

The Completion of Birth, Life, Death, and Rebirth

The Reunion of Our God Presence with the Beloved

The Original Creation of Eternal Life

Home

Diamond

I AM Complete.

Harmonic Resonance

Faceted Perfection of Oneness

Ascension

All

The Return to Love

"The full and true purpose of all life's incarnations is to prepare you to become a Sun of Light within yourself, free of the wheel of birth and death, and master of energy and vibration."

—Lord Sananda

To incarnate on Earth is a great honor and privilege. Our life lesson here consists of learning to transcend duality so we can return to the nondimensional realms of Light, or *ascend*. While we're on Earth, our soul's purpose is to be the greatest expression of Light we can be.

We live in an incredible time when opportunity for Ascension is available to everyone. It wasn't always so readily attainable, and we've never had so much help as we do now.

Read on.

Ascended Masters
and the Spiritual Hierarchy

A great Spiritual Hierarchy has guarded and guided us through eons of time. This Spiritual Hierarchy—also known as the Ascended Host of Light and the Great White Brotherhood—is composed of Ascended Masters and Beings. The Ascended Masters lived on Earth, just like you and me. They learned and mastered Universal Law and attained their Ascension as real and tangible beings. Jesus, Mother Mary, Buddha, and Archangel Michael are a few you may know who belong to the Great White Brotherhood. When they ascended, instead of moving into the higher spheres of perfect Harmony, Peace, and Love, they chose to remain in the denser realms to assist us. However, Cosmic Law states the Ascended Masters are not permitted to intrude upon our free will or offer assistance unless specifically asked to do so.

In the late 1930s, the Spiritual Hierarchy—acting as messengers and helpers of the Directing Intelligence of God—issued a special dispensation. This allowed information and spiritual instruction to freely flow from the Ascended Masters and the

Archangelic realms to humanity. Since then, we've been gifted with writings, messengers, and channeled information to assist in our evolution. In addition, gifts abound from the mineral and plant kingdoms to help increase our awareness.

When we consciously choose and realize Ascension, we connect with All That Is, or God. However, even with help from our spiritual guides, each of us must do our own inner work and evolve to meet the requirements for Ascension.

Now, with opportunities for heightened consciousness, we can realize and integrate the Divine Principles of the Ascension Codes to sustain these vibrations of *Peace on Earth*. In Harmony, there is no resonance for the denser energies of discord, lack, and suffering. They simply can't exist.

As we manifest more perfection, we create more Light and Love for ourselves and others. This can be described as the New Age, the New Earth, and the return of the Golden Era. We can be enlightened and in an ascended state of consciousness while still embodied in the physical realm.

It was not always this way. In the past, when an individual qualified for Ascension it was necessary to raise the physical body into the Christ Self, and then ascend into the I AM Presence, as Jesus did. Prior to the ability for the physical body to hold a greater Light quotient, Spirit had to separate from the body in order to ascend. Now the purified essence of the physical body is drawn into the etheric body and then the Ascension into the I AM Presence takes place. The outer structure of the physical form remains.

Spiritual and healing gifts are now available to facilitate the body's transition from the density of carbon to a crystalline structure, which holds more Light. Thus it's possible to be in an enlightened consciousness and still maintain a physical form. That means we don't need to give up the physical body to ascend.

In Truth, we become *descended masters*. Lord Jesus demonstrated this when he returned in his full Vesture of Light after his own resurrection. As the *risen* Christ, Jesus could choose to appear in physical form or not. And when he did appear in human form, it was in his perfect crystalline matrix, not in the cellular structure common to dimensions of duality and polarity.

What Is Ascension?

Ascension means the atomic structure of the physical body returns to the purity of its origin. This pure atomic structure is called the Adam Kadmon. When the atom moves back to its origin, it becomes pure Light and Love once again. Ascension happens when the critical mass, or Light quotient of the physical body, becomes greater Light and Love than the density of Earth's physical plane.

Ascension involves embracing and remembering our Divinity. Where did I come from? Why am I here? Where am I going? It defines who we truly are, what we call our I AM Presence. It necessitates expanding the meaning of Love. It also requires living life from the Wisdom of our Heart, which results in a new way of *being*. Therefore, we must bypass *thinking with the mind* and integrate *living and learning through the Heart*. After all, if our knowledge stays in the realm of the intellect, it's merely information that's not incorporated into our being through experience.

The word *Ascension* is sometimes misunderstood because of its Christian religious connotation. In a religious context, only Jesus, the *only* begotten son of God, had the supremacy to ascend. Dogma decrees that only Jesus can ascend, but not you, an ordinary human being.

In the context of *spirituality,* Ascension means simply being free from all energy created by the misuse of free will. We are all *sons* of God accessing our own Divinity. Jesus was showing us an example of what's possible, living fully as our God Presence in a physical body on Earth. Our physical bodies now have the capability to hold increased Light consequently allowing us to *ascend* and still remain in physical form. This, in effect, creates greater opportunity to serve mankind. In essence, we become masters of energy and vibration through aligning with the Love and Wisdom of God. We can thus carry forth our spiritual work at the highest levels of evolution.

Wisdom of the Heart

The way to self-discovery is found in Jesus' message:
"Seek and you shall find; knock and it will be opened to you."
Matthew 7:7

Spiritual seeking is the first step to accessing higher dimensions. First, however, we must *know* that other dimensions exist—that Universes lie beyond Universes, exceeding our limited comprehension. Intuitively, we have always known this. Today, the world's astronomers, physicists, and scientists are quantifying and proving what was considered science fiction only a decade ago.

The full revelation of Truth remains ever present. Truth never changes; only our narrow awareness limits our understanding. Our evolving consciousness enables us to discern greater details in Truth. To the degree that we can absorb and realize Truth, it is "true" to us.

Wisdom's way is through divine experience. We receive Wisdom on the level we can comprehend. Only after we become consciously aware that these higher realms exist *and we're able to resonate with their vibration* can we access the realms of Light and Love.

If we have a common resonance, then we can integrate higher frequencies with our own energy. If we intend for our lives to have limitless joy, Peace, and abundance, then we can start by expanding our knowingness and increasing our openness to receive these blessings. We seek answers, go within, and receive our guidance—Wisdom of the Heart.

The quest and the answer become one.

The Law of Acceptance

When we experience an *aha* moment, it excites us to awaken. We take note and observe—another step on the spiritual journey. Scientists are discovering that simply by observing, we can manifest change. However, observing will take us only so far. As an observer, you aren't the realized Self, and you can only imitate what you see. You may *see* the Light but not *be* the Light.

An accelerated process is available through the Law of Acceptance and the use of the Ascension Kis.

The transference of consciousness from one mind to another is called *education*. Searching through books, attending seminars, and following a guru will educate you but may not reveal higher Wisdom to you. Once you're consciously aware that higher realms of Light and Love exist, you're influenced by the Law of Acceptance. That's when the observer becomes the acceptor and education becomes knowingness. This point of conception reflects the union of the Divine Mother and Holy Spirit with the Source of Creation. When you open to the Law of Acceptance and transition from *observer* to *acceptor,* you attune to the vibration of Light and Love. You merge with it. You become it. I AM that I AM.

The Ascension Kis are spiritual tools that help you access your Divinity.

Sacred Resonance

The only way we can *be* or even *observe* Light and Love is to tap into the same frequency with which they're vibrating and hold a similar resonance in our being. Only then can Light and Love cross the threshold into our being.

Ascension Kis are bridges to Wisdom—from Earth to the highest cosmic realms. Some of the kis contain both higher notes and lower notes. Often, we're required to take steps before attaining the full Light of the ki.

For example, consider the ki called Freedom. Freedom's frequency vibrates lower than its higher vibrational complement called Liberty. Freedom is the first step, or level, to the attainment of Liberty. Freedom releases the boundaries of confinement, dissolving any belief in a limited existence. Once those limited beliefs are surrendered, Liberty expands the consciousness to everything beyond those boundaries and offers the Freedom to be everything. Some people will have to master Freedom before they can access Liberty. Others will be able to directly connect with the consciousness of Liberty without taking the step of Freedom.

We all enter the frequency of the kis at our soul's level of comfort and evolution. Levels of kis expand into higher and higher consciousness. The Ascension Kis create a vibratory frequency that allows Divine Principles to merge with the physical, mental, emotional, and spiritual bodies.

Sound simple? Well, here's the challenge.

When we experience these high vibrational frequencies in our four lower bodies, they may feel unfamiliar to us. Often, our first response to the unknown is fear, doubt, or resistance. We fear the unfamiliar and resist or rebel. Lovingly, our Higher Self nudges us along. In time, bolstered by faith and Trust, we lessen our resistance and once again venture into the higher realms to start exploring anew. Little by little, as we become more familiar with and attune to this vibration, we release our fear and uncertainty. Then we remain a little longer in this new vibration, becoming more at ease. Ever so slowly, we spiral toward the realms of Light and Love, transcending the dimensions of duality.

After all of our seeking, asking, and knocking, we come to know the existence of other Universes and higher realms of consciousness. We come face to face with our Higher Self—our I AM Presence, our God Presence. And we yearn to *be* the greatest expression of Light we can be—*now!* We know it as we acquire an insatiable thirst for Light and Love.

What Are Ascension Kis?

The Ascension Kis (pronounced "kees") are sacred, multidimensional tools gifted to us for our spiritual Earth journey. They're spiritual symbols that originate from the language of Light, a sacred geometry that's a Universal language transcending all time, space, and dimensions. This sacred geometry, embedded in our DNA, creates a *knowing* that goes beyond our conscious comprehension.

Kis are perfect and free of distortion. Each ki symbolizes an Ascension Code. Together, they attune to our Higher Self, the Christed I AM, our God Presence, bringing our physical, emotional, mental, and spiritual bodies into balance with pure Oneness. The kis create a resonance we can readily integrate without resistance or rejection, allowing us greater access to Light and Love.

The symbol *ki* is a portal, an opening. Its sound and meaning are similar to the English word "key," as in a *key* to open a lock, a *key* point or essential fact, or the perfect tone and resonance of a musical *key*.

The concept of time and space is specific to a certain level of consciousness. It may be a necessary step to understanding the full realization of nonlinear reality, or the Circle. Whatever your truth and understanding, the Ascension Kis will communicate with your Higher Self at that level of your awareness. As you continue to accelerate your evolvement beyond time and space, you will transcend these limited beliefs. Then through the kis—omni-dimensional vibrations of Light and sound—Spirit will communicate with your Higher Self in the consciousness of total Oneness. Each ki communicates to your soul's level from your God Presence to your human awareness.

Kis form a link to our Higher Self so we can become cocreators with Spirit. They synchronize opportunity, choice, and matter into an explosion of Grace, Light, and Love as they uniquely open a pathway to Ascension.

How Do Ascension Kis Work?

Symbols and sacred geometry are woven into the tapestry of life. They compose the architecture of physical form. All beings who make Earth their home—angelic, human, and elemental—can evolve into higher frequencies of vibration and consciousness by using Light language. Each symbol in the Universal language of Light communicates to a higher plane of consciousness within the human psyche. When we actively engage with the Ascension Kis, these symbols can open the gateway of Wisdom for the mastery of Divine Principles—a mastery necessary for Ascension.

We each have a divine blueprint that reveals our unique contribution to God's divine plan and guides our destiny. Our individual blueprint is created from sacred geometric symbols, our key to communion with God within. With help from the Ascended Masters and through contemplation with the kis, we can begin to master the Divine Principles as we apply this Wisdom to fulfilling our destiny so we may gain Freedom and Ascension.

Ascension Kis are tools for daily spiritual practice. Each Ascension Ki vibrates at a specific frequency that holds the essence of a Divine Principle synchronously resonating with your own energy field. In Harmony with the Divine Principle, your physical, mental, emotional, and spiritual bodies are balanced with the highest level of attunement and awareness you can hold. The Ascension Kis connect to Oneness/All That Is; the messages contained in the symbols are nonlinear and omnipresent. With practice, Wisdom becomes conscious and bestows on us the gifts of Grace—serenity, poise, dignity, opulence, beauty, perfection, and balance.

You learn to live in Love.

The organic energy in the kis powerfully adapts to myriad levels of consciousness. Kis are held in all dimensions, not being of any particular dimension nor limited to souls advanced on their spiritual path. You'll receive the vibration of Oneness appropriate for you and will never be overwhelmed by too much energy or information. Each time you master a Divine Principle, the kis reveal a new awareness and higher consciousness. The kis' dynamic alchemy resonates with your unique blueprint and harmonizes their frequency to the level you're ready to receive. They resonate with every aspect of your soul in all dimensions where it resides. When you integrate the kis' higher frequencies into your present awareness, their vibration will begin to benevolently spiral you into gifts of higher consciousness.

In addition to being a portal, each Ascension Ki is a bridge of Light. The vibration of the kis transmutes any form of resistance into pure Source energy. If you experience a lack of clarity or unknowingly accept misinformation of the true codes that hold God consciousness, these sacred geometries will transmute, recalibrate, and balance that energy. In your meditation, the kis will open planes of consciousness for all Divine Principles to flow into usable form. Then, through your individual awakening, you become a catalyst for others to receive the Ascension Codes.

Guidelines for Using Ascension Kis

Unless you can apply the Wisdom of the Universe in practical and useful ways, it remains theory—unusable. How can you take the indescribable and make it understandable? How can you move from the intelligence of the mind to the Wisdom of the Heart?

As you meditate with each Ascension Ki and master each Divine Principle, you will experience divine Grace, Wisdom, and "Peace that passeth all understanding" in your life. By working with the Ascension Kis, you can activate the process of remembering in many ways, usually in the following order:

1. Conscious acknowledgement
2. Intellectual understanding
3. Letting go of *thinking* with the mind to *feeling* with the Heart
4. Living each Divine Principle through thoughts, feelings, and actions
5. Simply *being*

Through practice with the kis, a process will unfold in which your I AM Presence will open you to the profound spiritual gifts that are your divine right and inherently yours.

As this experience becomes part of your personal journey, it's up to you how you wish to use the Ascension Kis. Allow your intuition to guide you. Your intention alone will help integrate the energy of the kis into your life.

As you begin to use them, you may experience a feeling of uncanny familiarity with the symbols, a kind of *déjà vu*. It means your inherent, intuitive knowing that transcends your mind and connects you to your Higher Self is remembering. Like all of us, you have divine Wisdom within you—Wisdom you've simply forgotten.

The Ascension Kis help you remember your I AM God Presence, who you truly are—a magnificent God Being.

Start Your Practice

Y ou may find it helpful to have a journal and pen nearby to record any messages you receive or feelings you may experience.

You needn't follow any particular order or sequence of kis. Start with a ki you feel familiar with or know the meaning of. For example, you may not have a good sense of what Harmony is, but you might know the feeling of Gratitude. Start there. Or simply flip through the pages of this book and start wherever you land. One ki will lead to another; one Divine Principle will support the next, revealing glimpses of what is yet to unfold.

When you've chosen the ki you wish to practice, read its accompanying information and affirmation. Once you've "intellectually" engaged the essence of the ki, change from *thinking with your mind* to *feeling with your Heart*. Doing open-eye meditation, contemplate the sacred geometry as if you're taking a photograph with your third eye. Allow the energy to flow past your mind, bringing the feeling and energy to your Heart.

Once you feel the energy of the Divine Principle moving into your Heart, imagine in your mind's eye that you're projecting the symbol into your energy field. When you feel ready, make an invocation, say a prayer, or state an affirmation. Charge it with Love and Allow its energy to do its perfect work through you. Allow yourself to fully feel the energy of Light and Love and the interconnectedness of All That Is.

Life is a journey. The path is infinite and eternal, continually spiraling, connecting to the Heart of God/Goddess/All That Is. The Ascension Kis can help you open to the spiritual process of Ascension.

JOURNEY OM.

In Gratitude

Peace Waters and the Journey OM series of books—*Journey OM, A Soul Journeyer's Adventure, The Soul Journeyer's Companion,* and *Ascension Kis*—are all divinely directed writings of inspiration.

In the creation of *Ascension Kis,* I am grateful to Elohim Peace and Aloha, the Ascended Masters, Saint Germain, Lord Sananda, and Lady Nada, Paul the Venetian, Serapis Bey, and the Great Divine Director. I am also grateful to Archangel Michael, Gabriel, and all of the Archangelic Messengers who guide me in Love and service. Peace Waters would not *be* without your Wisdom and devotion. I am humbled to be your dedicated chela.

I am especially grateful to the Ascended Master Teaching Foundation©. This organization continues to publish and distribute a library of channeled Wisdom devoted to individual Ascension and world Peace.

Thank you to the artists in my life, James Gordon Kelly IV and Mike Clark. James found in his heart the Source of creativity that inspires his art. He has gifted us with the ability to *see* Light and Love in the whimsy of his character "Moto" and the precision of his sacred geometric kis. Mike creatively transformed thoughts and words into a cover design that inspires readers to open the pages of all the books in The Journey OM Series. His fine art in oil and acrylic transcends the limits of the mind.

To my soul companions Judith K. Moore and Ahriah Vocare who share the Wisdom of the Ascended realm as clear channels of Light. They give words to my feelings, allowing me to share divine guidance and inspiration through Peace Waters and through my writing.

Thank you to everyone who answered the call and contributed their expertise to produce this book so I can be free to craft my ideas into words: Barbara McNichol, editor; Karen Saunders, publishing consultant, project manager, and book interior layout; the MacGraphics Services team of dedicated professionals Kelly Johnson and Helena Mariposa.

I am grateful to my teachers, friends, and family for making my life experience rich in Spirit. And most dearly, I dedicate all of my *being* to my beloved husband, Jim Kelly, whose love and inspiration surround me in all time and space.

I share Peace. I share I AM in Oneness with you all.

I Am So Grateful!

A Special Acknowledgement

In this lifetime I have been gifted with a soul team, a group of individuals who come together and support each other's divine purpose. Judith K. Moore and Ahriah Vocare are two of my divine friends. Long forgotten and way before this lifetime we agreed when the time came for New World Peace we would join together as Ascension wayshowers and assist each other in our spiritual service. That time is now.

The Ascension Kis are Peace formulas channeled by Judith from Elohim Peace. Working with Ahriah and the Ascended Masters I deepened my understanding of the kis and embraced the vision of bringing these spiritual gifts into form. In 2007 when James Gordon Kelly awakened to his gift of artistry everything was in place to write, illustrate, and print the first booklet and deck of cards. Over the last few years, we have individually followed our spiritual paths and deepened our understanding of the Ascension process. As we evolved more kis were revealed. I personally dedicate this book you are holding to my friends Judith and Ahriah.

Judith K. Moore

Judith K. Moore, lecturer, author, visionary, and cosmic oracle is dedicated to the New World of Peace. She has authored four books translated in English and Dutch; and three more, soon-to-be-published books. She is a global traveler guided to sacred sites where she clears and opens energy centers. Equally as important as her work with Mother Earth is the heart connection she makes individually with the local people. Supporting the ideology of *unity in diversity,* Judith believes that "Peace will come when people meet each other heart to heart."

Judith is a conscious trance medium and adept. Opening to the stored Wisdom of Creation in the Akashic Libraries of Light, she communicates these transmissions solely for the highest good. As the sacred cosmic oracle for The Records of Creation, an organization dedicated to heal and activate the world grid for birth into the New World of Peace, her calling is to serve as a divine messenger to awaken the critical mass.

Judith is the mother of six children, all who were lovingly adopted; and grandmother and great-grandmother to many, many more. Judith is an ordained priest in the Eastern Oriental Orthodox Catholicate Church of St. Thomas and holds her PhD in Therapeutic Counseling.

Judith has dedicated her life to Spirit's calling. It is an act of faith and a journey of love.

Ahriah Vocare, MA

"You are made in the Light to live and breathe the Light. The Spirit and Love that shine through you is yours. Do not hold back this Light; give it to the world. Open your windows and doors and let it shine on all mankind. You belong to all. You have been called to share the Light. Answer the call."

— Lord Ashtar

This was Ahriah Vocare's first channeled message, which affirmed her calling as an Angelic and Ascended Master channel. She believes her message from Lord Ashtar is also meant for you.

Ahriah's exploration of God and self started early, in Catholic schools. Two earned degrees—a BS in Education and MA in Psychology— expanded her knowing beyond the boundaries of dogma and initiated her search for deeper understanding. That's when Ahriah's teachers appeared from India, Egypt, and Australia.

In 1987 Ahriah enrolled in a *How to Channel* class and the Ascended Masters and Angels began to speak through her. She had found the direct connection she had been seeking. Soon after, she received her Spiritual name from Lord Master Serapis Bey— Ahriah—*bringing God into form.* At last, she had discovered her life's calling.

Ahriah is a life coach who teaches seminars and offers private channeled sessions. She considers herself privileged to support her clients by connecting them to their spiritual guides and angelic messengers.

Contributors and Resources

Ascended Master Teaching Foundation

www.ascendedmaster.org

P.O. Box 466, Mount Shasta, California 96067

Mike Clark Fine Artist and Designer

In Mike Clark's words, *"I hope my paintings convey a calming sense of place, one of peace, that relieves the viewer—at least for a moment—from the cerebral discord caused by the instant, over-saturated, technological clutter of a modern world."* This is the heart and soul of Mike's passion for painting and design. A Montana artist, Mike graduated from Montana State University in 1988 with Bachelor of Arts degrees in Fine Art Drawing and Graphic Design. He has uniquely integrated these two disciplines and his work has earned him award and publication. Mike hopes to deliver a product worthy of your time and appreciation.

You can contact him at mclark2721@hotmail.com

James Gordon Kelly IV *(See About the Illustrator)*

You may contact him at jgkiv@mac.com or jamesgordongallery@gmail.com.

Kelly Johnson

Kelly Johnson works with authors and coaches to manage technical, creative, and administrative projects for their businesses and books. She's an article writing coach, does blog and website maintenance, implements online shopping cart strategies, and is the principal of Cornerstone Virtual Assistance. She can be reached at kjohnson@cornerstoneva.com, and her website is www.cornerstoneva.com.

Helena Mariposa

Helena has been proofreading for fourteen years. She became curious about e-books when she received a Kindle, and she has been creating e-books ever since. She won an EVVY award for her work with e-books. In addition to running Mariposa E-book Transformation, she continues to write and proofread professionally. To learn more go to her website: www.booktransformation.com, or email: helenamariposa@comcast.net.

Barbara McNichol Editorial

Barbara McNichol Editorial provides expert editing of articles and nonfiction books in the categories of business, spirituality, self-help, how-to, health, relationships, and more. Over the past twenty years, Barbara has placed more than 300 books on her editing "trophy shelf."

Barbara also helps authors, speakers, and entrepreneurs improve their writing through her monthly ezine *Add Power to Your Pen* and her Wordshops: How to Strengthen Everything You Write. She is the creator of *Word Trippers: Your Ultimate Source for Choosing the Perfect Word When It Really Matters.*

You can contact Barbara at 520-615-7910 or editor@barbaramcnichol.com. Please visit www.BarbaraMcNichol.com and/or connect on LinkedIn, Facebook, Twitter, and Google+.

Judith K. Moore *(See A Special Acknowledgement)*

Judith offers private sessions to persons on their spiritual path who are ready to realize their living blueprint for their ascension process. Sessions can be scheduled by signing up on her web site.

Author of four books: 1) *Song of Freedom—My Journey from the Abyss,* 2) *Visions of Wisdom—Messages from the Council of the Thirteen Grandmothers,* 3) *A New Formula for Creation—the Miracle of Immortal Love,* 4) *Crop Circles Revealed—Language of the*

Light Symbols (coauthor Barbara Lamb). Books available in Dutch, coauthored with Herbert van Erkelens: *Mary Magdala—Prophetess of the Living Covenant* and *The Mirror of Magdala.*

Visit her website at www.recordsofcreation.com.

Karen Saunders, MacGraphics Services

Karen Saunders is the owner of MacGraphics Services, a unique design firm for today's entrepreneur. Karen's team of award winning designers, editors, illustrators, and support personnel help small business owners publish their books, build their brand, launch their website, and market their business. By creating polished brands, dynamic graphics, and compelling content, the MacGraphics support team has successfully elevated many speakers, coaches, and consultants to the next level. Karen's own book, *Turn Eye Appeal to Buy Appeal: How to easily transform your marketing pieces into dazzling, persuasive sales tools!* won the 2007 CIPA (Colorado Independent Publishers Association) EVVY "Best of Show" book award.

You can contact her at 303-680-2330 or karen@macgraphics.net, or visit her website at www.MacGraphics.net.

Ahriah Vocare, MA *(See A Special Acknowledgement)*

You may contact her at spiritshift@earthlink.net.

About the Author

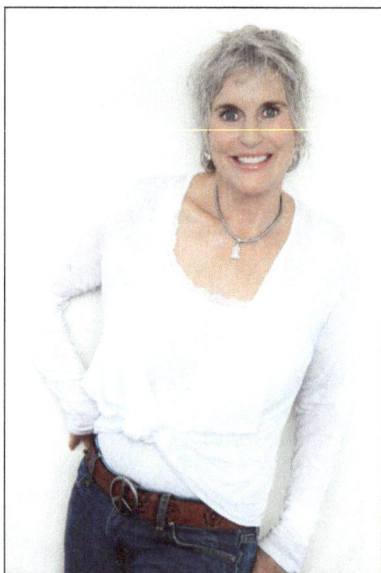

Shima Shanti

Life's experiences have touched Shima Shanti in profound and unexpected ways. During her careers as a corporate executive and then an entrepreneur, the vision of a *future memory* led Shima to realize the world is ascending to a higher vibrational consciousness. As she gracefully opens to enlightenment, Shima has been deepening her understanding of the Ascension process through gifted resources, intense study, and insight from the spiritual realms.

On her path of self-discovery, she came to know her God Presence embodied in her physical being. Realizing she was no longer bound by old karmic patterns, she found her spiritual freedom and embarked on her path of service as an Ascension wayshower.

Since then, Shima has answered Spirit's call to adventure, traveling the Western

United States, Canada, Portugal, and Spain. She has followed both established pilgrimage routes and spiritual retreats, including Chief Joseph's Trail, Archangel Michael's etheric Temple of Faith, and the *Camino de Santiago de Compostela*. Each journey has deepened Shima's self-realization of God.

Of these travels, nothing was more profound than her walk through Portugal and Spain in 2012. Alone, in a foreign country, with nothing but a backpack and herself, she walked nearly 500 kilometers in unyielding rain. That's when she accepted the challenge to fully surrender to *All That Is*. The heart-searching solitude she experienced gave her a clear understanding of her divine purpose. It has evolved into her own *Camino*— and her next call to serve.

Shima's soon-to-be published book *The Camino of Shima Shanti* is the revelation of Truth and unveiled mystery told through her *Camino* journey. As this Light-minded soul says, "I'm always ready for the next tap on the shoulder to serve."

The author has been writing creatively for more than twenty years. With her husband of thirty-eight years, she and Jim balance their lives between San Diego, California, and Whitefish, Montana, contrasting walks on the beach with hikes in the high mountains. They fully savor the simple actions of life through the enthusiasm of their grandson Micah and their Maltese pup Star.

About the Illustrator

James Gordon Kelly IV

Life and Spirit in perfect balance—that peaceful feeling that exists when we connect to our core essence, centered and empowered. It is the gateway to creativity. In that creative space resides James Gordon Kelly IV, son, husband, father, artist, and PGA professional.

Gifted with a natural athletic ability and a keen intellect, childhood successes came easily to James. Boredom caused by his "taken-for-granted" talents led James down a path of self-discovery that was not true to his core essence. Now, having rediscovered who he is through his creativity, his life and Spirit are in perfect balance. And his art shows it!

Through meditation, he quiets his intense intellect and athletic competence to allow the direction of his soul to guide him. This is the source of his artwork. Whether he's capturing his subject's soul essence in a portrait, exposing the beauty of still-life nature, collaborating on book illustrations, or bringing the magic of mystical symbols to light, his artwork is inspired by the four elements: Earth, Water, Wind, and Fire.

James is grounded by his Divine Principles: Patience, Presence, Divinity, and Oneness. His art follows his journey on the path of his personal discovery—one that is just beginning.

Also by Shima Shanti

The Journey OM Series

Book I: Journey OM, A Soul Journeyer's Adventure

This story of Peace and Freedom recounts Shima Shanti's pilgrimage to link the constellation Pleiades and the National Historic Chief Joseph Trail to the New Age of enlightenment. *Journey OM* will touch every reader in some way—10,000 years ago, in 1877, or now.

For many, *Journey OM* delivers an interesting read about a misunderstood historical exodus. For those who are ready, the book holds spiritual lessons, Light codes, and Universal Truth. For everyone, following this journey will expand your consciousness and open you to the Oneness of *All That Is*.

Book II: *The Soul Journeyer's Companion, A Cosmic ReMemoir*

In this supernatural story, Shima Shanti fulfills the quest for Peace and Freedom unrealized by Chief Joseph in 1877. She is guided to go to Lake Louise, cradled in the

Canadian Rockies. There, spiritual remembrances reveal her path to enlightenment and the homecoming of her soul.

The Soul Journeyer's Companion, written from a soul's perspective, is about experiencing the fullness of Divine Self as a physical being.

www.ingramcontent.com/pod-product-compliance
Lightning Source LLC
Chambersburg PA
CBHW040740150426
42813CB00064B/2962